About Demos

Who we are

Demos is the think tank for everyday democracy. We believe everyone should be able to make personal choices in their daily lives that contribute to the common good. Our aim is to put this democratic idea into practice by working with organisations in ways that make them more effective and legitimate.

What we work on

We focus on six areas: public services; science and technology; cities and public space; people and communities; arts and culture; and global security.

Who we work with

Our partners include policy-makers, companies, public service providers and social entrepreneurs. Demos is not linked to any party but we work with politicians across political divides. Our international network – which extends across eastern Europe, Scandinavia, Australia, Brazil, India and China – provides a global perspective and enables us to work across borders.

How we work

Demos knows the importance of learning from experience. We test and improve our ideas in practice by working with people who can make change happen. Our collaborative approach means that our partners share in the creation and ownership of new ideas.

What we offer

We analyse social and political change, which we connect to innovation and learning in organisations. We help our partners show thought leadership and respond to emerging policy challenges.

How we communicate

As an independent voice, we can create debates that lead to real change. We use the media, public events, workshops and publications to communicate our ideas. All our books can be downloaded free from the Demos website.

www.demos.co.uk

First published in 2005
© Demos
Some rights reserved – find details of the Demos open access
publishing licence at www.demos.co.uk/openaccess

ISBN 1 84180 146 1
Copy edited by Julie Pickard
Typeset and produced by Land & Unwin, Towcester
Printed in the United Kingdom

For further information and
subscription details please contact:

Demos
Magdalen House
136 Tooley Street
London SE1 2TU

telephone: 0845 458 5949
email: hello@demos.co.uk
web: www.demos.co.uk

Everyday Democracy

Why we get the politicans we deserve

Tom Bentley

DEMOS

Contents

Acknowledgements

This piece of work is the result of a collective effort by many colleagues and friends at and around Demos over the last four months. All the staff at Demos and many of its trustees and associates have taken part in a series of conversations which have formed and strengthened the argument. Those conversations in turn have been part of a much wider process through which Demos has developed its principles and priorities. Those involved are too many to mention, but thanks to Eddie Gibb, Paul Skidmore, Duncan O'Leary, Julia Huber, Neal Lawson, Shelagh Wright, Sophia Parker, Claire Ghoussoub, Abi Hewitt, Sam Hinton-Smith, Paul Miller, James Wilsdon, Jake Chapman and Bob Tyrrell for contributions that have been essential to completing the work. That said, every one of my colleagues has contributed in some way to the idea and its expression. Finally I must thank Kylie Kilgour and Esther and Iris Bentley for distracting, putting up with and inspiring me in equal measure.

The text reflects a perspective on where our democracy is, and why it matters. But it emerges from a much wider range of practical work and exchange in which Demos is involved, in a growing number of places. Its purpose is not to define the answers, but to open up a wider conversation about how we govern ourselves and our world, and how we can learn to do it better.

Tom Bentley
June 2005

Summary

Overview

Democracy is facing a crisis, but simply reforming the structures of governance will not lead to democratic renewal. The public needs to take an active part in the renewal process.

Everyday democracy means increasing public participation in the formal and informal institutions that shape our daily lives. People should be able to make individual choices in ways that contribute to the common good.

Renewing democracy through public participation increases our collective capacity to tackle major problems facing society, such as the pensions shortfall and climate change. Many of these problems can be addressed only by changing the way we live our daily lives.

Demos is committed to building everyday democracy. This essay concludes with some principles for building everyday democracy that Demos uses in its work with organisations in the public, private and voluntary sectors.

We get the politicians we deserve

Our confidence in political leaders is declining, but when we opt out of political processes altogether we make their leadership less legitimate. In Britain, poor voter turnout and reduced party membership have created the conditions for political instability.

Without a working democracy, we will be unable to adapt to the social and economic pressures of globalisation.

Britain's 2005 general election did not renew the legitimacy of the prime minister, and both main parties are moving towards selecting a new leader. But too much faith is put in individual leaders to restore the legitimacy of their parties and the health of democratic politics as a whole.

Politicians need to renew their own parties and help to increase wider political participation if our democratic institutions are to work effectively. But if we, as citizens, choose not to play a part in this process of renewal, we will get the politicians we deserve.

Everyday democracy

Liberal democracy combined with market capitalism has reinforced the tendency of individuals to act in ways that reduce our ability to make collective choices. This is the underlying reason for the crisis in democracy.

Democracy should be a way to balance personal rights and shared responsibilities, with political institutions mediating between individual and group interests. But political institutions seem irrelevant to people's daily lives, so their ability to mediate is reduced when we need them most.

The solution is to reconnect democratic choices with people's direct experience of everyday life, and to extend democratic principles to everyday situations and organisations.

Crisis? What crisis?

Faith in political parties is declining across Europe and trust in politicians seems to be at an all-time low. Political campaigning is now conducted largely through the media. Politicians are in the public eye but politics are not part of people's everyday experience.

There is pressure on politicians to act as they try to convince sceptical voters to support them. Creating consensus about tackling major problems, such as the pensions shortfall or climate change, which require public behaviour change, has become very difficult.

Where are the leaders?

Our political culture perpetuates the myth that strong leaders can bring about change single-handedly. But the developed world has few examples of leaders who have successfully converted their formal authority into a process of democratic renewal.

Rather than relying on the authority of office, real leadership means motivating people to solve problems for which there are no easy answers. These principles for leadership could help societies adapt to new challenges:

- Acknowledge the limits of existing solutions.
- Allow solutions to emerge from different sources.
- Distribute power to people who can solve a problem most effectively.
- Refuse to be diverted and learn from failure.

Where are the citizens?

People are too busy for formal politics, though many are involved in informal political activity ranging from volunteering to NGO campaigns. Participation is distributed unevenly across the social groups, creating a sliding scale of citizenship.

In Britain there have been several recent responses to this gathering crisis in democracy. They include:

- the POWER Inquiry, which is looking at ways to increase participation
- a renewed interest in electoral reform, including a campaign for proportional representation by the *Independent* newspaper
- the Hansard Society's commission on parliament and the media, which called for greater transparency.

However, these responses may focus too much on reforming political institutions. Constitutional reform is only part of the solution. Democracy must also be embedded in the everyday reality of people's lives.

The role of deliberation

Most of us form our views based on our own experience. Institutions that are not connected to the everyday experience of people are unlikely to have much popular support.

Conversation, or deliberation, is an important influence on people's views. When institutional decision-making fails to connect with people's experience, they do not feel ownership of the process and are less likely to take part. The European Union is the obvious example of this.

The challenge for democratic renewal is to create opportunities for deliberation that relate to both people's experience and collective decision-making.

Markets and democracy

The triumph of markets at the end of the twentieth century is widely misinterpreted as meaning that the state struggles to create public goods or influence markets.

However, the idea that markets and the state can be kept separate is misleading. For one thing, markets depend on legitimate governance to work effectively. And for another, good governance depends on the interaction of many institutions – including ones that are part of neither markets nor the state.

Most importantly, though, people do not experience any separation between state and markets in their daily lives. For people to make choices that are not purely consumer choices, markets and the state need to be more integrated, not more separate. Institutions that govern markets should be more democratic.

Choices and commons

Commons are resources which are freely accessed and shared, but are often essential to private interests too. Many of the problems we face in our society stem from the fact that we do not see a connection between our personal choices and the commons on which those choices depend.

Using plastic bags at supermarkets or driving children to school are everyday examples of personal choices where the wider consequences – social, environmental or economic – are not properly acknowledged.

So governance exists in part to protect commons. But our argument about democracy reaches further: democratic legitimacy is itself a common good that enables us to solve problems together as a society.

We will solve shared problems only when people are persuaded to accept a share of responsibility for them and the public value of collective problem-solving is recognised.

The role of institutions

We need institutions to help us see personal choices in relation to the common good. Elected governments are just the tip of the iceberg. Traditional institutions commonly grouped under the heading of civil society are also part of the picture.

But non-traditional institutions also contribute to the common good. Parental childcare networks and book clubs are two everyday examples. For these self-organising institutions to play a different role in mediating democratic choice, their development must be combined with the uses of state power.

The most practical way to link individual choice to collective responsibility is to participate in the institutions that influence our lives. Formal and informal institutions should be democratised, and given more responsibility for exercising state power.

Building everyday democracy

Demos has committed itself to building everyday democracy by applying the principles set out in the above analysis in its work with organisations from all sectors. There are four main ways to develop institutions as the basis for everyday democracy:

○ Develop public services and local governance as platforms of self-governing communities.
○ Recognise membership and campaigning organisations that can play a clearer role in mobilising political issues and mass participation.
○ Support institutions that can enable cultural learning and collaboration between cultures.
○ Spread institutional power more widely and seek to align power, initiative and responsibility more closely.

These challenges cannot be met through existing structures of government. But the British government could stimulate more everyday democracy by developing the local roots of democratic self-governance. This could be done by:

○ creating a local government financial settlement which localises a significant proportion of tax-raising power and matches powers to responsibilities
○ embracing neighbourhood governance which delegates management and budgets across key areas
○ embedding public deliberation in institutional development such as trade negotiations, scientific research and innovation programmes, and land development
○ reshaping public services to make co-production by citizens as important as professional knowledge and performance management
○ involving citizens in local government budget-setting processes.

1. We get the politicians we deserve

The British general election of 2005 has shown that political legitimacy is hard to come by. It did not renew Tony Blair's authority or transfer legitimacy to any other leader. Instead, it revealed a barely contained public hostility towards professional politics. More people chose not to vote (39 per cent) than voted for the governing Labour party. More than half of the public describe *both* the Prime Minister and Leader of the Opposition as 'untrustworthy'.[1]

Any national election is a specific judgement of particular parties and their leaders. But this one also marks the re-emergence of a longer-term pattern which is reflected around the world: the steady decline of trust in politics and attachment to its institutions. The form of nation state democracy that dominated the second half of the twentieth century is holed below the waterline. People are withdrawing from its rituals and routines. But democracy cannot work on the people's behalf without their active consent.

In Britain, we hope the coronation of new political leaders will 'put things right'. But it is our democratic system that is at fault and is creating a crisis of governance. We go along with the myth of strong leadership until those leaders – almost inevitably – fail to live up to expectations. But when this happens we question only the leader, not our faith in the myth itself, which is perpetuated by the media-based way we consume politics.

But the perpetual cycle of hope and failure of strong leaders hides the fact that our democratic system is at fault and we face a crisis of governance. Our politics duck the big and difficult issues like climate change and pensions reform, but at the same time seems unable to put right even small things. So it is not just new leaders, but a new democratic settlement, that we need – a paradigm shift in the way we do democracy.

The decline of deference is not a bad thing, but when it sweeps away all kinds of public legitimacy we have a fundamental problem. That's why I say that we get the politicians we deserve, because our opt-out from politics inevitably reduces the legitimacy of leaders. In an age when people feel they have better things to do, we need to work out how to set public rules that allow us to live good lives together.

Over the next generation our societies will have to negotiate profound transitions in social, economic and cultural life. Yet our popular assumptions about sovereignty apply nineteenth- and twentieth-century methods to twenty-first-century problems. Changes to governance, law and regulation are happening, often at the transnational level, but they are largely disconnected from everyday life.

So while our societies are wealthier, healthier and more open than perhaps ever before, there is a collective crisis of confidence about how to hold them together and adapt to change.

Democracy, though an ancient idea, is a relatively recent achievement. In different parts of the world, it is vulnerable to poverty, violence, corruption and exploitation. We have to recognise that the dramatic rebalancing of power going on after the end of the Cold War, and the sudden expansion of the global market, requires both fledgling and mature democracies to reinvent themselves.

Democracy should allow us to adapt, without violence, to new realities, according to the best possible ideas we can come up with about how to live. For a century in Western Europe, the preferred way to do this has been through party competition and universal suffrage. Politicians compete to tell stories that offer a narrative of hope or reassurance, while we project our aspirations and anger onto them.

However, the basis on which politicians make their stories believable is collapsing as our scepticism increases. The danger is that a growing gap between political elites and everyday experience will become a vicious cycle, narrowing the range of choices that politics can offer because it cannot mobilise people to change their behaviour.

The erosion of fragile democratic cultures will lead to the breakthrough and dominance of a far more basic and violent form of identity politics. The existence of far right parties in Europe, and of radical Islamic parties in many other countries, illustrates this possibility.

The fundamental question for twenty-first-century politics is how to combine market economies with other kinds of value – social, cultural, environmental, public and moral – in ways that sustain our societies and our natural environment, and align economic production with human need.

Our shared problems and challenges include:

O   how to socialise and educate children, spread opportunity and offer proper care to a burgeoning elderly population

O   how to manage the new frontiers of scientific knowledge and power, and to negotiate the close co-existence of different cultures and religious faiths

O   how to respond to new sources of economic competition and create the foundations of future prosperity

O   how to reverse climate change and protect biodiversity

O   how to build cities and suburbs in which everybody can thrive

O   how to achieve security without compromising justice, and how to address the scale and depth of global economic inequality.

These are major challenges of collective adaptation – they need large-scale solutions, expertise, institutional rules – but the new solutions will also rely on mass changes in individual behaviour and on value commitments, not just technical requirements.

To adapt successfully means making public rules and institutions *legitimate* in a context where obedience to institutional authority is breaking down and personal freedom is creating ever greater social, cultural and ethnic diversity.

In this essay I argue that there is only one logic that offers a way to reconcile these tensions: the logic of democracy. Without renewing democracy at every level, our capacity to succeed as societies, and then as individuals within them, will drain away. Without new forms of democratic sovereignty, innovative and creative changes to our current model of political economy will not emerge. Without the mass exercise of citizenship many of our public traditions and institutions will atrophy. Without a new level of direct citizen participation the legitimacy of our political institutions will continue to decline. Without new cultures of dialogue, exchange and learning, our social differences will overwhelm us.

That is why democratising the relationships between people, institutions and public authority is the central challenge of our age.

2. Everyday democracy

Liberal democracy, combined with market capitalism, is supposed to have triumphed at the end of the twentieth century. But its brief honeymoon soon found it awash with new challenges. Not only has liberal capitalism created a world in which jobs can be exported by corporations, and terrorists can strike through communications networks, but the specific forms of freedom that Western citizens now enjoy have led to increasing disdain for the constitutional models that brought them about.

Not enough people see democratic politics as part of their own personal identity to sustain the cultures and institutions through which political legitimacy is created. The result is that our preoccupation with making individual choices is undermining our ability to make collective choices. Our democracy is suffocating itself.

Yet a public realm, in which all can participate freely, equally and through which different identities and cultures are mediated and respected, is a precondition of liberal freedoms.[2] Recognition of this problem has led a stream of philosophers to focus on the need for shared responsibilities amid a world of private freedoms.[3]

Swelling their ranks is a growing number of religious and civic leaders concerned both at the effects of unrestrained markets and individualism on more vulnerable members of society, and at the dangers of retreating from a shared public culture. Thus Rowan Williams, Archbishop of Canterbury, recently warned that we risk neglecting the full needs of children because of our preoccupations with consumption, while Chief Rabbi Jonathan Sacks has called for religious communities, including Jewish ones, to resist 'turning in on themselves'.[4]

Alarm bells are being rung, too, by those focused on the wider systems of order and renewal on which survival depends – from Martin Rees, British Astronomer Royal, calling us to avoid making this 'our final century' to scholars like Jane Jacobs and Jared Diamond – questioning whether human societies have the capacity to foresee and avoid catastrophic collapse.[5]

We need to renegotiate the basis on which we share responsibility for this public realm – the wider context in which ordinary lives are lived out. Democracy is the only set of principles that can allow us to do this – enjoying personal rights demands collective responsibilities, which in turn require new rules of governance.

The question is how this set of principles can be given tangible expression through institutions that connect with people's daily lives, rather than being imprisoned within cultures and institutions that are viewed only through the long-distance lens of the media. Only if democracy is anchored in everyday experience will it be possible to legitimise shared rules that restrict people's freedom some of the time. For that to happen, people must share in both power and responsibility.

But they must do it in a world where everyday life can be flexibly connected to an amazing array of cultures, places, organisations and activities, where structured working and gender roles in stable local communities are a rarity, where global flows of ideas, culture, money and people make the connections between personal choices and collective outcomes increasingly hard to fathom.

The concept of everyday democracy allows us to reconfigure democracy for this age. It is the practice of self-government through the choices, commitments and connections of daily life. Everyday democracy means extending democratic power and responsibility simultaneously to the settings of everyday life. It relies heavily on the mediating role of institutions that can symbolise and represent shared commitments – but simultaneously stimulates a wider range and choice of such institutions. It means that people can actively create the world in which they live.

Around the world there are growing examples of everyday democracy which point to how democratic principles and participation can become embedded in ordinary life, not just formal political structures. The Mondragon network of cooperatives in the Basque region of Spain, owned and governed by its members, employs over 60,000 people, provides skills and management training for all of its workers and gives 10 per cent of its profits to social causes.[6] In British Columbia, Canada, a Citizens' Assembly made up of ordinary people is enquiring into the reform of electoral systems.[7] At the Semco manufacturing company in Brazil, workers vote on how much they should be paid.[8] At the Bromley by Bow Centre in East London the doctors in the health practice pay rent to their patients through a community trust. In the Brazilian city of Porto Alegre, residents take part every year, through a network of meetings, in setting the city's budget priorities.[9] In South Korea, OhmyNews.com uses 'citizen reporters' as contributors to its online news service, taking named reports from more than 20,000 member-contributors.

Democracy in this context is not so much a form of government as a set of principles for structuring the interaction between diverse participants, given the combination of autonomy, diversity and interdependence that people and organisations exhibit.

Democracy cannot flourish without being guaranteed and practised by the state. But in open, networked societies, the interaction between public and private goods goes far beyond what the state can directly control.

Building everyday democracy therefore depends on applying its principles to everyday institutions through which people make their choices and develop their identities. Its basis is the idea that power and responsibility must be aligned with each other – and widely distributed – if societies are to exercise shared responsibility through social, economic and institutional diversity.

We can learn, through practical innovation, how to build

organisations and decision-making systems that support these requirements. But the essential lesson of democratic history is that unless the maintenance of political structures is combined with deepening cultures of democratic participation, democracy will fall apart. The solution is not simply to create more direct democracy, or to set up an ever-growing array of consultative processes divorced from the exercise of real power, but to embed both these principles – direct and deliberative – in the range of institutions through which people can express their concerns, their needs and their identities.

Understanding how to strengthen a sense of membership across a wide range of institutions, and then how to factor those institutions into the use of state and public power, is the key to revitalising people's participation in political and civic life.

3. Crisis? What crisis?

One symptom of collapsing identities is the fact that, in country after country, political parties appear to be dying on their feet. Fifty years ago in Britain one in ten of the population belonged to a party. Now fewer than one in 40 do. Parties are struggling to recruit members, field activists and retain a respected role the world over. A 2004 Eurobarometer survey of the 15 pre-enlargement member states found 76 per cent of respondents saying that they did not trust political parties (compared with 61 per cent for big business and 46 per cent for religious institutions).[10]

Since 1974, the proportion of British people saying that they trust the government 'always or mostly' has fallen from two-fifths to one-fifth.[11] Perhaps even more significant, however, is the broader social pattern of people's hopes and fears – 58 per cent say that they are optimistic about their own personal futures, compared with 9 per cent who admit to being pessimistic. But when asked about the direction of society as a whole, the balance is very different. Only 23 per cent are optimistic, compared with 43 per cent who are pessimists. This pattern is repeated consistently across the industrialised world. It betrays a striking lack of confidence in the social and institutional environment.[12]

This is not automatically a problem. The fall-off of political parties might not be a surprise, given the collapse of the cold war ideological divide, the growth of media power, the range of other ways in which people can spend their time, and the rise in wealth and education across much of the world. If successful government is a question of management and stability, then the decline of parties might be welcome.

But we have to ask – as parties become shrunken rumps of their former selves, focused on marketing political brands in an increasingly competitive media market, but unable to provide the permanent bridge between national institutions and street level social reality – which institutions will take their place in mediating between the experience of individuals and the uses of government power?

The first answer is that, in information-drenched societies, a free media plays this role. And on one level this is obviously true. But journalists are among the few groups of professionals trusted *less* than politicians in many countries. The competitive dynamics of media culture helps to project politics as a constant battle in which the task is to expose, to embarrass and to scrutinise the governing classes on the assumption that such pressure is the only thing that keeps them honest. This dynamic has helped lead political culture into a cycle of antagonism which is further undermining the possibilities of politics as a whole.

Electoral dynamics, in a postideological age, encourage parties to crowd towards the centre, and the cultures of media scrutiny, political attack and consumerism combine to push difficult collective choices, however important, away from the immediate political agenda.

As voters have come 'closer' to politicians through the impact of television and electronic media, familiarity has bred contempt. After the Second World War, more than 90 per cent of Britons agreed that it was a 'serious neglect of one's duty' not to vote. In 2001 less than half agreed with the same statement.[13]

In response to the demand for sensation and drama, politicians have moved further towards the culture of attack and response, vying to create 'moments' of drama which cut through the cynicism and distraction that dominate attitudes to what they do. One party leader described the experience as a 'daily battle' to come off best in a struggle that would be reduced to ten seconds of tape on the television news.

But, as it heads further in this direction, politics is fighting a losing battle against forms of theatre and spectacle that are more entertaining, and forms of conversation and social exchange that are more meaningful to citizens. There is a clear analogy with football, which has been affected in similar ways by the changes of the last 20 years.

What began as an amateur game has been professionalised, televised and globalised to the extent that a few key personalities dominate the global pecking order.

The drama of football is extended by a relentless focus on personal battles between managers and the shadowy activities of agents and proprietors. The influx of attention and money has created a relentless focus on the performance of teams, in the full glare of a 24-hour media. But the wider value of professional football depends far more on the vitality of football culture in parks, schools, playing fields and amateur leagues than on the attempt to squeeze more excitement and drama from the Premier League.

Even more pertinently, Premiership clubs could find sustainability in mutualisation – defining participation in the club through shared ownership that excludes the drain of payments to external financing and maximises the commitment of the audience that helps create the whole event. What is presented to a global television audience as a spectator sport actually rests, in the long run, on mass participation and shared ownership.

As voters fall away into anger and indifference, the ability to create consensus and legitimacy for difficult decisions becomes even more remote, creating a vicious circle with no obvious way out. The looming pensions crisis is a perfect example. We know we are spending too much now and saving too little for later. Collective action and government intervention is necessary to create a solution. But while politicians fear the electoral backlash of intervention and fail to create a consensus on what needs to be done – nothing is done.

The effects of globalisation have made the tasks of political leadership and government more difficult, at the same time as public culture has become less deferential and more demanding. Media culture, the new Opposition, becomes ever more intense and unforgiving, scrutinising from every conceivable angle. Domestic issues, from jobs to food safety, are influenced by global forces which politicians must be seen to grapple with but awkwardly have to skirt around. Real global security concerns like organised terrorism have to be addressed without political leaders losing their grounding in 'national concerns'. Issue-based campaigns like Make Poverty History find ever more visible and sophisticated ways to set the public and media agenda. In every field, effecting change means influencing increasingly complex sets of actors and rules through interventions whose effects are largely unpredictable. Yet politicians must show continuously that they are 'making a difference'.

The professionalisation of politics, and its focus on influencing powerful elites through networks while communicating simplified messages to targeted swing voters through television, has encouraged the conclusion that politics is a parallel universe, separated from ordinary life and somehow corrupted by the rules of its own game.

So despite political issues remaining high, and perhaps even increasing, the sense of distance between public and high politics is palpable. As Andrew Cockayne (of MORI) puts it, 'people confess to being too immersed in their jobs, families and leisure time to get involved in the detail'.

4. Where are the leaders?

These conditions have meant that leaders, as individuals, are even more pivotal to the focus and progress of politics than ever before. But in focusing on the performance and character of public leaders, we risk exacerbating a set of conditions which undermines their ability to fulfil any promise at all.

Politicians use narrative as their most potent weapon. They try to tell a story that captures people's sense of what is happening around them, their aspirations for the future, and their sense of anger or betrayal at the status quo. In the process, they hope to associate the teller of the story with a sense of trust and capability which they use to build their authority.

The ability of leaders to project and communicate a sense of purpose, renewal and progression has become pivotal to their perceived political success. But looking around the Western world it is hard to find an example of a political leader succeeding in the leadership of sustained political or wider national renewal. From Gerhard Schröder in Germany to Vladimir Putin in Russia, Paul Martin's imploding minority government in Canada to Goran Persson's struggling Social Democrats in Sweden, the ability of leaders to generate clarity, momentum or legitimacy when facing challenges of transition is surprisingly weak. Even George W Bush, simple in his message and politically dominant, is finding it surprisingly difficult convert the 'authority' of leadership into radical institutional change.

Given the heights of political dominance which Tony Blair once enjoyed, it was probably inevitable that New Labour would come to be viewed as a disappointment. Tony Blair has suffered a backlash, which often arises when a leader is seen to override or manipulate public opinion, over Iraq, just as Margaret Thatcher eventually did over the poll tax. But while the public can both praise and punish 'strong' individual leaders, our public culture continues to overemphasise their ability to change things single-handedly.

As Ronald Heifetz of the Harvard Kennedy school argues, leadership is not synonymous with the holding of authority, whether formal or informal. Leadership is a process through which a wider community is mobilised to meet a new challenge or solve a problem. Yet the incentives and pressures on politicians, amid today's politics, are often to *avoid* confronting the public with issues or challenges that they might find uncomfortable.[14]

Tony Blair's career has not been short of uncomfortable challenges, from reforming Labour's clause 4 commitment to nationalised industries to addressing antisocial behaviour to galvanising an armed intervention in Kosovo to Iraq and now to climate change. But it is striking how far his damaging disappointments have arisen from not being able to generate sustained, institutionally grounded strategies through which to succeed in these projects. As Geoff Mulgan, founding director of Demos, recently wrote, 'Britain still awaits a radical reformer who can recast the state to cope better with big issues like environmental change, poverty or localism.'[15] His analysis points to the importance of institutions over policies in generating or frustrating deep change, but still risks over-reliance on the leader as a source of radicalism.

In the absence of both traditional authority and coherent ideology, our political culture is making the punishment of failure for such leadership far too great for ambitious politicians to contemplate it. If political leadership is unable to bring about long-term shifts in the orientation of institutional life, and through it personal behaviour, then it cannot do its job.

Yet despite these difficulties, the next round of domestic politics in

Britain will be dominated by leadership speculation – how would Gordon Brown be different as prime minister? who could lead the Conservatives out of political wilderness?

It is incredible that the Conservative Party has had to take a step *back* from democracy in its own leadership selection process in order to avoid the perceived extremism of its own members' views. But it also shows that, right from the clause 4 moment and possibly earlier, party reform has been presented as leadership for long-term institutional renewal, when the reality has been much closer to effective political management – creating the conditions for a successful takeover of an existing institution, but being unable to create conditions in which it could prove attractive to grass roots members, be capable of generating policy or organisational innovation, or create any wider legitimacy for its leaders in more difficult times. Modern political parties in Britain have done none of these things in the last decade.

In contrast, Greece's new opposition leader, George Papandreou, has actively looked for a different set of principles in setting out to renew his PASOK party and the basis on which he would campaign for government. Papandreou has conducted an open conversation with members and other Greeks which has involved 150,000 people putting forward their views about what politics should do. Rather than succumbing to the pressure for instant answers, Papandreou has set out an open process and emphasised the importance of creating diversity *within* political parties if they are to represent wider society.

For the sceptical times we live in, a new set of leadership rules is emerging, superseding traditional command and control politics. To address the adaptive challenges effectively, we need leadership which:

○ identifies problems and challenges for which there are no easy answers, and communicates powerfully our need to share responsibility for them
○ acknowledges the limits of existing solutions without retreating from the problem or abandoning it to private interest

○ mobilises people to participate in creating solutions, and includes diverse participants – insiders and outsiders, enthusiasts and resisters – in the construction of a solution

○ uses authority to create a 'holding environment' in which solutions can emerge from different sources, rather than demanding instant, comprehensive answers

○ distributes power and resources to those places and people who can most effectively solve a problem

○ sustains a focus on the issue over time, refusing to be diverted by distractions or opposition, and shows itself capable of learning from failure and partial success

○ models honesty and clarity in a way that seeks to encourage others to practise the same.

To make politics work, political leaders must be able to focus on problems that they do not know how to solve, and mobilise people to generate long-term solutions. To do this successfully leaders need a form of authority rooted in the *ethical* imperative for addressing the big challenges that face society. Their approach needs to be based on the values that matter in developing the solution, rather than simply the exercise of command or the certainty of conviction. If we accept this, it should also be obvious that the prospects for more successful political leadership also depend on the consent and participation of citizens.

5. Where are the citizens?

So where are all the citizens? The Electoral Commission estimates that there are 15.5 million political conversations in Britain every day, and that 57 per cent take part in at least one discussion of local issues. Around half a million people a year give money to Oxfam – probably more than the membership of all political parties combined. Levels of protest and activism, at least among the educated and well off, have risen slightly. The range of social movements and campaigns through which to engage in political action has never been as broad. MORI recently found that more than half of the population says it is very or fairly interested in politics, and over three-quarters is interested in national or local issues.

But deep 'immersion' in the details of everyday life means that people's routines are dominated by work, family, friendship networks and entertainment. On average, people spend just four minutes a day volunteering, compared with over two hours watching television and video.[16] One reading of these changes is to say that, for those who are confident enough to do it, party politics matters less because they have so many other channels: wristband campaigns, international NGOs, local action groups and so on.

The decline of formal political participation is uneven in its impact. Up to a third of people in socioeconomic groups D and E say they do not take part in *any* kind of political or campaigning activity, including voting. The distorting effects of this distribution on political priorities will only get worse, as parties try to target wavering middle class votes at the expense of those worse off but voiceless.

Effectively, this means that citizenship works on a sliding scale; your level of education, confidence and income has a direct impact on the extent to which you access, and influence, politics and the public realm. As an individual, our ability to access the opportunities and the protection of democracy is correlated with our economic power and social status. As a recipe for fairness or legitimacy, it does not look good.

Recognising this, responses are beginning to appear to the vulnerability of democratic politics. In Norway, the national government commissioned a five-year project on power and democracy. In Britain, the Rowntree group of independent charitable bodies has supported a POWER inquiry focused on the decline in democratic participation.[17] The *Independent* newspaper has begun campaigning for electoral reform. The Hansard Society's commission on parliament in the media, led by Lord Puttnam, has pointed out the need for greater transparency and better communication of what parliament does.[18]

These responses are crucially important, but they share a common risk – that they will end up focusing too much on the institutions that we currently have, and not enough on the wider conditions and cultures under which participation becomes meaningful. Take voting reform. It is arguable, of course, that the disproportionate relationship between seats and votes obscures the legitimacy of elected governments and distorts our political culture towards 'all or nothing' competition. But Australia, which has one of the most sophisticated proportional representation systems in the world, combining single member constituencies with transferable votes and including minority parties in its upper house, is suffering from exactly the same democratic shortcomings.

Politics is not separable from daily life. The forms of engagement that people choose (or don't choose) are embedded in the circumstances and routines of their own lives. How can we separate our political perception from our consumption of television and media? How can we separate our sense of justice from the experiences of those we regularly spend time with? How can we distinguish our ability to influence events from our experience of family, school and working life?

This is the basic shift in perspective that we need in order to renew democracy: we have to discover how to build institutions that reconnect this everyday experience with shared outcomes that work at the scale of today's world. An issue like climate change will be addressed only when the strategy works simultaneously at every level from personal to global, and these levels will be aligned only through action taken through nation states. But for this to happen, personal responsibility and political choice must be enacted *together*.

In other words, for our democracies to thrive, we must stop discussing them as if 'the public' could be herded back into a pen and convinced to follow the routines and obligations of a set of external institutions. Instead, the institutions and their principles must become endogenous – embedded in the fabric of everyday life, influencing the nature of everyday interactions without pre-determining their outcome.

Example 1: A democratic media?

The media is the classic example of institutions whose independence from state control is fundamental to democratic freedom but whose collective claim to 'self-regulation' has increasingly tattered its collective behaviour and impact. The ownership of media industries, from newspapers through television to the internet, clearly affects the composition and influence of the way they report, but so does their culture and internal market structure.

The competition for market share is intense, to say the least, and yet many media organisations follow distinctively national territorial boundaries. What would a more democratic media look like? In South Korea, OhmyNews.com has pioneered a new kind of news service, in which users are also contributors, filing copy, checking stories and taking part in online dialogue and discussion.

The principle of citizen contribution changing the dynamics of content production can also be applied to the regulation of media organisations for accuracy. Geoff Mulgan and Tom Steinberg recently proposed a new institution: the Open Commission for Accuracy in the Media (OCAM), dedicated to promoting accuracy in the media and providing information about news channels and media organisations, complaints against them, peer review tools through which to check reputations and adjudications and so on.[19] The argument is that open knowledge sharing and interactive media make it possible to use citizen power to help regulate media organisations without having to channel it through the vertical authority of a state regulator.

6. The role of deliberation

The decline of institutional authority means that people are less prepared to recognise what they are told from above as a way to guide their own behaviour. What they *experience* directly is much more likely to influence their sense of who they are and what matters in life. This might help to explain why people are more likely to say that they trust doctors, teachers and newsreaders to tell the truth rather than politicians, journalists or business leaders.

Yet the more powerful this personalised perspective becomes, the more distant and diffuse are the institutions and rules that have made individualism possible. In his concept of six degrees of separation, Stanley Milgram showed that through social networks any two people in the world could be connected in six or fewer easy steps.[20] The same is true of the connection between our everyday decisions – what to buy, whether to travel by car, which employer to work for, how to discipline our children – and the global issues that shape our collective quality of life. But in this case the 'degrees of separation' are often presented as layers of governance. Through these systems the connections between power, responsibility and action inevitably become lost from the citizen's view.

This is a major source of the disconnection between personal choices and collective consequences, or between political decisions and personal experience. What the citizen, the service user or the customer sees is often very different from the objective of the organisation or the reality experienced by those taking decisions in them. Both the processes used to organise the service and the wider effects of the interaction are lost from view.

The sense of being controlled or influenced by distant forces over which there is no control or accountability leads directly to the forms of protest and backlash that can be seen in today's anti-political movements, whether it is the British National Party attacking immigration, network-based protest movements like ATTAC challenging the symbols of economic globalisation, or resistance to the apparent encroachments of the European Union on identity and shared values.

The European Constitutional Treaty is a classic illustration of this, whereby the democratic deliberation going into the design and negotiation of the constitutional treaty – a new set of governance rules designed to improve outcomes for citizens in an enlarged union – was conducted at such an elite level that it has become entirely separated from the exercise of direct democratic choice over it, which comes through national referendums. When people are presented with such an elite and remote 'choice' it is little wonder that it becomes a backlash against the political establishment rather than a collective consideration of vital shared interests.

As Amartya Sen, among others, has argued, a narrowly economistic view of citizens' preferences fails to account properly for both the practice and the potential of democratic decision-making.[21] People take account of a broad range of information when they are making such decisions, and public discussion – conversation – has a major influence on their eventual choices.

Where direct experience is separated from the deliberative process, a sense of membership and influence over the outcome is quickly lost, however sophisticated the process. This is one reason why so much innovative democratic thinking has gone into generating new forms of deliberation, through citizens' juries, assemblies, deliberative polling and so on.[22] But the experiments often have in-built limits – either they are not sufficiently connected to real power to have any purchase, or they are enclosed by location and scale, and therefore have little leverage on wider public attitudes or political culture.

While economists are right that people have consumer preferences, and political theorists are right that freedom to choose one's own version of the good life should be respected and protected, the reality is also that people's views and behaviours are highly adaptive. Not only do they change over time in response to circumstances, but we are heavily influenced, consciously and unconsciously, by what others around us think and do.[23] Given this, the process of deliberation – of public discussion among citizens – is fundamental to the possibility of democracy, and 15.5 million daily conversations suggest that it has strong roots. But part of the challenge of everyday democracy is to establish how deliberation, responsibility and individual participation can be connected with, and embedded into, the exercise of power.

Example 2: The democratic family

The role of the family as a social and economic unit is pivotal to the success of the economy, to people's wellbeing, and to wider social structures and order. Yet the place and status of the family in public life is surprisingly ambiguous, and the difficulty of establishing a consensus around its preferred form is great.

This most private set of relationships has a startlingly public significance. Parenting could be seen as the most important public responsibility, given the consequences for others of damaging parental relationships. Yet the boundaries between privacy and public intervention remain vague, and the effect of law on practices such as divorce, smacking, domestic violence and parental equality is uncertain. Government therefore struggles to find methods of intervention that are genuinely effective and legitimate in influencing outcomes without invading privacy.

However, treating the family as a democratic unit, sharing responsibility and practising how to meet shared needs through negotiated differentiation of roles, appears far more viable than reliance on any other model of hierarchical authority, or of treating the family as a loose collection of self-interested individuals who may opt to exit at any moment. Thus parents may assume different economic and household roles at different times, but aim to share equality of status and power in the relationship.

Children are treated as having equal worth and special rights, despite being unable to exercise full individual powers for themselves. In practising dialogue, negotiation and distributive fairness, family members are training for the allocation of roles and resources in wider life, as well as often adapting more spontaneously and flexibly to changes in family circumstances, household technology and so on. The habits of consumption, saving, learning, emotional resilience and communication that children develop within families have a profound impact on the shape of their adult lives, and therefore on the wellbeing of others and their cost or contribution to the future economy. Treating family relationships as part of a conversational democracy might lead to a new understanding of their place in wider society. Clearly, families are not fully democratic communities; children do not and should not have full decision-making rights. But nonetheless, society, helped by evolutionary psychology, should strive to ensure that parents put children's interests first. Giving children votes to be exercised on their own behalf by their parents until the 'age of majority' could make a start at enshrining their place in a democratic society.[24]

7. Markets, dynamism and democracy

Another reason for the perceived decline of politics is the growing power of global markets. A recent Eurobarometer survey of people living in the EU found that 64 per cent of respondents agreed that globalisation concentrates power in the hands of large companies at the expense of others, 57 per cent agreed that globalisation represents a threat to employment, and only 39 per cent agreed that, overall, globalisation is 'a good thing for me'.[25] The same survey found that only 19 per cent trusted governments to control the effects of globalisation, and only 7 per cent trusted political parties to do so. Despite this, the conventional wisdom that states have lost power is not really true. While the boundaries of their control are much more porous, most national governments spend as high a proportion of GDP as they did 30 years ago.

In every period of history, the form and function of the state has changed to reflect the nature of power and the kind of social contract needed in order to achieve security in the world and legitimacy among those who abide by laws, pay taxes and fight in wars. The Magna Carta was written to provide constitutional guarantees, in return for the funding of war by landowners. The postwar welfare state provided comprehensive social protection and full employment in return for the collective sacrifice and loyalty required to win total war.

As Philip Bobbitt has shown, this integral connection between external strategy and domestic order is the key to understanding how states have changed through history. He argues that since the end of the Cold War we have seen a rapid shift away from welfare states, towards a 'market state' committed to maximising opportunities for citizens, but leaving it to the interplay of markets, choices and autonomous organisations to shape the eventual outcomes of those possibilities. This means that, in the economic, security and cultural spheres, 'the nation-state faces ever increasing difficulty in maintaining the credibility of its claim to provide public goods for the nation'.[26]

In Britain, this kind of shift is evident in New Labour's approach to social policy, where it has deliberately sought to invest in skills, opportunities and prevention, rather than using direct economic control and income distribution as its main forms of intervention. Labour has consistently made a case for public investment to help bring about an 'opportunity society' as Tony Blair recently described it.

But if legitimacy is part of the aim, then the market state description alone is not complete. The victory of free-market thinking was so great that governance is still treated as an inefficient restraint rather than a springboard for legitimacy and innovation, even on the left.

Instead, the unspoken assumption is that only market exchange can stimulate innovation. Thus governance, in the corporate as well as the public sector, is seen as a 'dead hand', creating layers of stifling control and bureaucracy which divert resources from their most productive uses and introduce 'politics' into organisational life. This governance effect is perfectly possible; indeed, it often results from market failures and crises, as companies, governments and other institutions use compliance with risk management processes to insulate themselves from liability.[27]

But, either way, the danger is that both centre-left and centre-right end up trailing behind the effects of economic change in their attempts to make public interventions. This is one reason why New Labour's political strategy of achieving economic stability and then increasing public investment has shown only patchy returns in citizens' perceptions. A second problem is that the effects of economic growth – more hours worked, more retail developments and so on – continue to change the social landscape which frames people's experiences and choices, but their ongoing, dynamic effects are not integrated fully into the plans and decisions of government. Society is forever trying to play catch-up with the market.

This problem applies to right and left alike – both are searching for a convincing account of how the public and private realms can be combined sustainably. For centre-right social morality, whether liberal or traditional, it is still hard to see how appealing to personal responsibility and voluntarism to protect public goods like the environment, or to address social exclusion and poverty, are anything but running against an unstoppable tide.

In open, globally exposed societies, we are slowly getting used to the reality that markets cannot be contained by structural separation of sectors – institutions and areas of life cannot be walled off from the influence of competition and choice. But collectively we still need ways in which to identify, create and protect forms of value that markets and marketing do not account for.

Simply arguing that government is investing in the ability of its citizens to thrive as individuals in a global market is unlikely to convince most people. Even where governments have successfully intervened through redistribution they are often reluctant to claim any success for fear of alerting those who may have lost out. The politics of stealth ends up making no one feel good about the process – but crucially fails to build legitimacy and consensus for further reform – creating a glass ceiling for political action.

This does not mean that governments can return to direct provision, control or coordination of health, education, labour markets, broadcasting, childcare and so on. It means that politics must find more decentralised and self-organising ways to invest in the creation of public goods.[28]

Markets and governance have been in a symbiotic relationship for centuries. As Robert Cooper puts it, 'the driving forces of globalisation may be economic, but its foundations are political'.[29] Trade follows peace, and the institutions of government grew out of the shared commitment to ending and preventing war. The problem is that the boundaries of markets – global networks – are now out of kilter with the strongest forms of governance – nation states – with predictable consequences for legitimacy.

However, it is just as important to recognise that governance and democracy are not identical. The rapid evolution of global governance through treaties, regulators, transnational rules and so on – of which the European Union is an exemplar – is progressing without strong or direct democratic participation. But the drift towards populating new governance institutions with a technocratic elite, only weakly connected to the exercise of popular sovereignty, is generating its own forms of backlash – both through open defiance and through the leaking away of public attachment and loyalty.

This creates a common problem. Market economies cannot thrive without legitimate governance. Societies cannot thrive simply by letting the cycle of market innovation set the cultural, political or public agenda. But without deference to institutional authority, governments will struggle to enforce those rules that they are responsible for maintaining.

For democracy to be meaningful it must be able to generate a range of alternatives – a public ready to endorse and support the options, and institutions capable of organising them in the face of other pressures. But it cannot do this when it is walled off into a separate, and shrinking, set of organisations and activities. The possibility of choosing other kinds of value – time, friendship or tradition over market goods or pressures – needs to be legitimised through collective dialogue, and practised by enough people to make it viable. Democratic choices depend on critical mass, on the existence of a 'multitude'.[30]

Democracy can be a source of dynamism and creativity when it distributes power, responsibility and initiative widely across different communities and organisations and makes it possible to compete and collaborate over a wide range of possible solutions. The question is not how to separate the two domains from each other, but how they can become better aligned so that public and private forms of value can be rebalanced.

As Bobbitt argues, the transition to a market state involves the nation state relinquishing its claim to provide goods on everyone's behalf.[31] But many of the goods on which democracy depends are not created through direct state control. Instead, they emerge from the conjunction and interaction of a much wider range of institutions and communities. Innovation in governance occurs through the existence of a much more pluralised range of institutions and relationships which, through their interaction, make up the public realm. In the space between direct state control and private individual choice there exists a multitude of opportunities to build a shared public and democratic life – anchored in everyday choices, but shaping our wider context. The question is how to harness this range, which also supports personal identities and private choices, for the creation of common goods.

Example 3: Democratising work

Whereas the twentieth century was dominated by a culture of scientific management, the next century will be characterised by democratic management. This means a shift away from the industrial model, in which one person comes up with an idea, draws up plans to implement it, and then ensures that the workers carry out those plans efficiently and thoroughly. The most successful enterprises in the future will recognise that it is possible to grant members of an organisation more say over decisions, and make the cumulative quality of those decisions better. The best organisations of today are already doing this. This means governance structures for firms designed to maximise the value of distributed innovation and create stronger shared commitments to the enterprise as a community of members.

There are some examples of this in practice already. At Toyota, any employee can stop the production line if they have an idea that they believe will increase productivity or improve the quality of a product. The American army has become renowned for its review sessions after missions, in which the mission is evaluated and all members of the team – however junior – have license to step outside the established hierarchy and express their views. At Semco, the Brazilian manufacturing company, employees not only set their own salaries and job titles, but hire their own bosses. In each of these cases, the organisation is characterised by a culture of openness, and a recognition that the knowledge of the CEO is only a small part of the pool available to the company. At SouthWest Airlines in the US extensive employee ownership of the company is combined with very high levels of participation in management and coordination, with detailed performance information shared and used by flexible operating teams.[32]

8. Choices and commons

To reconnect personal choice with common good, we need to understand commons. Commons are resources which are freely accessed and shared, not subject to private property rights, but often essential to the successful pursuit of private interest. Commons are spaces that, in principle – anyone can enter – from the House of Commons to Wimbledon Common. But intangible commons – such as trust and knowledge – are equally important. The public realm can be understood as those places, resources and shared norms that are held in common by a whole society.

The most familiar discussion of commons and capitalism is, of course, the natural environment.[33] Protection of commons depends on enclosure – whether of grazing lands or intellectual property – to create enforceable, tradable, property rights, or to put the good under public protection, such as in a national park or museum.

Commons resources may sometimes be best protected by attaching price mechanisms to them – as with carbon trading – if they increase the incentives for valuing the resources being protected. So commons are part of a system in which markets can function well – but they help to create a category of resources which private property rights cannot easily value.

Perhaps the most important issue, however, is the extent to which everyday, personal choices in everyday settings have become disconnected from the commons on which the ability to make such choices depends. There are many familiar environmental examples: using plastic bags at supermarkets, driving children to school in private cars, taking cheap flights and so on. All are examples of personal choices where the wider consequences – social, cultural, environmental, economic – are treated as externalities and therefore not fully factored into the rules governing the decision.

So governance exists in part to protect commons. But our argument about democracy reaches further – that democratic legitimacy and collective problem-solving are forms of good that should also be valued as commons, because of the extent to which they facilitate successful and peaceful adaptation.

Common social goods, such as emotional wellbeing and trust, are one set of elements in a thriving democracy. Innovation – social and economic – depends on the existence of knowledge commons in which mutual learning through free exchange is collectively valued in a way that broadens access to knowledge and examples, reduces the risks of challenging received wisdom, and spreads the results of innovation quickly and widely for further testing and refinement.

In all these areas, everyday decision-making is an integral part of how the bigger system works. Whether the decision is how to bring up children, which newspaper to read, whether to drive to work, which loan to take out – the individual decision affects not just the market dynamics but the wider context in which it sits. Just as in the neoliberal critique of central planning – that no central authority could ever access the range of information used in decentralised market exchange – these personal and social decisions create cumulative impacts which either renew or run down our social commons. Yet in the vast majority of cases, the implications of the individual decision are unknown or unspecified to the person making the choice.

Legitimacy and respect for shared rules are also common goods – they cannot be owned by any one institution or participant, but they have collective value because they enable a wider range of choices and support. So the decision not to vote, for example, might be understood as the exercise of a personal freedom, but one which makes a tiny reduction in the legitimacy of the governing arrangements as a whole, and reinforces the voicelessness of the person who does so.

The argument, therefore, is that we need rules of governance that structure our everyday choices so that they can contribute to the creation and protection of common goods that we need to thrive, rather than leaving us ignorant, impotent or isolated in seeking to make the right choice.

Choice, and the freedom to choose, has of course become one of the sacred elements of the political landscape, a tenet of democracy and consumerism alike. Freedom of expression and self-definition are fundamental human rights and essential counterweights to the danger of political or cultural tyranny.

But the choices we make are conditioned by a whole range of factors; the meaning of choice will be different according to the context in which we make it.[34] Choice is a social phenomenon, embedded in a psychological, cultural or geographic context. For example, as Harvard criminologist Robert Sampson has shown, where people share expectations about the needs of young people in a neighbourhood, and are prepared to act on these expectations, health and educational outcomes are consistently better. Shared confidence in the ability to solve practical problems enhances the ability itself.[35]

Because of this, systems of organisation based on people making free choices can, at least potentially, be designed to make it possible for them to share responsibility, to participate in re-creating the context in which each individual choice is made. But to do this across different areas of life we need two things.

First, we need systems of decision-making and organisation capable of helping to make the choices visible, or transparent – to connect the act of individual choice with the wider, collective consequences. Second, we need to create regular opportunities for people to think, talk, learn and decide together about the issues over which they are making choices.

So the question is whether – in increasingly diverse societies and communities, where the imposition of external authority is both less influential and likely to be less legitimate – it is possible to structure rules and decision-making systems through which people can make everyday choices that meet their needs, reflect their identities and re-create the common goods on which their wellbeing relies.

The answer is a hopeful one. The source of inspiration for the possibility of self-governance in diverse, mass societies comes from the fact that, across the natural and social worlds, complex systems self-organise and adapt without central direction.[36] These models provide more than a metaphor; they are beginning to provide practical insights into the possibilities of shaping complex, adaptive *open* systems according to shared rules which have moral purpose and value.[37] This way of thinking about the evolution of social systems suggests that we should be looking to design institutional rules to encourage the *emergence* of common goods through the interaction between many autonomous participants, and that trust and legitimacy can be both a cause and a consequence of such emergence, though they cannot be taken for granted.[38]

However complex the system, the simple truth is that these shared problems will only be solved when people are persuaded to accept a share of responsibility for them – when the public value of their being solved is internalised, rather than externalised by markets and then ignored by individuals.

Political authority cannot insist on this internalisation. It depends on persuading people to make their own choices to support it, through parenting, driving, working, shopping, learning, recycling and so on. Political leadership can help to make it a public issue, but the solutions will emerge to the extent that we can develop institutions to underpin these behaviours.

Example 4: The London congestion charge

London's congestion charge, introduced by Mayor Ken Livingstone, illustrates the major elements of everyday democracy. First, it relies on enclosure of a commons – a zone with boundaries policed by camera. Second, by charging motorists it puts a tangible value on use of the commons – both road space during particular times and, by implication, air quality and carbon dioxide emissions. Third, it relies on a distributed participation by requiring users to take responsibility for paying. Fourth, it explicitly connects the revenue raised from the charge to investment in upgrading bus services, thus enhancing a public transport alternative which is universally accessible for almost all Londoners.

Democratising this governance arrangement further might involve linking payment systems and registration to involvement in user forums and co-governance arrangements, involving road users in providing information about delays, landmarks, speed cameras, bus routes and so on through an open access information system, and even moving to generative indicators that would provide real-time information about air quality, traffic congestion and travel to work times in different parts of the city through the day and night.

9. The role of institutions

The importance of commons then leads us on to the final stage of the argument – the recognition that without institutions it becomes impossible to protect and create common social goods. But thriving democracies are both cause and effect of these shared goods.

Institutions are the means by which we organise human activity at a manageable scale – big enough to be reliable and economical, small enough to be accessible, recognisable, have a human face and a tangible identity. And the institutions that people join and take part in through everyday interaction are the ones through which they express and develop their identities.

The institutions of direct state power and electoral representation are just the tip of the iceberg; they rest on a much richer ecology of organisational life, embodying forms of shared value which need to be protected, nourished and reproduced through everyday inter-action. This insight is hardly new. It has been repeated through social and political thought on both left and right for centuries, from Burke to TH Marshall and contemporary communitarian and systems thinkers.

But its modern expression – a general emphasis on 'civil society' – has led to far too weak an approach to the development of these institutions. Either they are romanticised (by elements of the right) as an alternative to the welfare state, returning to a more voluntary tradition of social provision which overplays their ability to counter the inequalities of class and markets. Or they are presented as an antidote to globalisation because they can mobilise anger and publicity through network-based activism. But neither of these extremes, nor much in between, can really stand up to the power of the nation state or the mega corporation on its own. For autonomous institutions to play a different role in mediating democratic choice, their organic development must be combined more systematically with the uses of public and state power.

The decline of traditional institutions that we discussed earlier is, in fact, matched by the spread of a wider range of much more flexible institutions, many operating in the market economy, which offer people access to experiences through which they can shape their identity. From software collaboratives to childcare networks, book groups to discount clubs, these self-organising forms offer channels through which people can connect to something bigger, often while meeting their own everyday needs.

The public realm has been marked by the development of institutions – from local government to universities, public parks to museums, childcare centres to professional associations – which offer a vehicle for shared identities. Institutions also take on new social roles – who would have foreseen supermarkets offering financial services, employers administering stakeholder pensions and football clubs hosting literacy classes, as part of their ongoing adaptation?

Institutional innovation, and the state's ability to prompt it and adapt to it, is therefore the major domain in which democratic renewal can be pursued. Where political reform or new governance institutions are being created, then the principles of both broadening and deepening public participation simultaneously must be the priority. Deliberative conversation – channelled through institutions that in turn affect the distribution of social, economic and political power – is the form of interaction which does most to generate the forms of trust, mutual respect and understanding that democracy requires.

It is through these multiple, overlapping attachments and forms of loyalty that people build up their picture of the world, and their sense of how they can influence it. It is by democratising the membership of these kinds of institution and giving them greater power in shaping the use of public power and money that people can access opportunities to practise the virtues and responsibilities of direct democracy.

Institutions adapt and innovate, decline and stagnate in response to changes in the social and economic tides around them. But to rebuild our democracies we must focus on the ways in which institutions – from football clubs to book groups, park management committees to workers' councils, astronomy clubs to gardening projects, youth centres, libraries and museums – create wider value and link people's behaviour to collective outcomes. The connections will be made at an everyday level, but the role of the state – and of democratic elections and decision-making – is no less important in learning how to influence and support the adaptation of these complex sets of organisations.

Example 5: The democratic school community

Schools, as community institutions, have among the highest levels of trust and social interaction. But schools in most industrialised countries are run as factory-like hierarchies with professional man-agement and vertical accountability structures, and their formal governance arrangement does relatively little to create wider public value. Some schools, of course, are formed by specific communities or by groups of parents in order to secure provision which does not otherwise exist. But all schools have much greater potential to act as a platform for the development of wider communities through shared use of buildings and shared learning activities designed to support children's development. In the process, they can also develop as democratic communities of learners.

This is already happening in many schools, supported by the government's policy of developing extended schools and funding out of school hours provision. But the wider potential of the policy is far from fully developed, given the range of other community learning institutions, family resources and other activities that could be linked together. Schools can also become partners in wider forms of community governance – partners in regeneration, hosts of community dialogue and platforms for civic leadership.

10. Building everyday democracy

Some principles for political renewal

We are at a moment where the power to interpret and impose a version of democracy is one of the most potent and potentially dangerous factors in global politics. Simultaneously, the world faces a challenge of framing shared principles through which it can negotiate its economic, environmental, political and military rules without triggering catastrophe.

Exporting a narrow version of democracy along with markets could be disastrous. But democracy should be understood as part of a capacity for self-organisation, and one of the conditions necessary to generate a wider range of political economy models for the twenty-first century. Its shape in different places will turn on its interaction with older and more powerful cultures, and with the effects of economic development; it is not a simple prescription guaranteed to succeed.

Rather than clinging to a tattered model of constitutional democracy whose purchase on our lives is reducing daily, we should be investing in the evolution of new democratic institutions and practices which, in conjunction with revived constitutions, can underpin sustainable, self-organising societies.

But how should such an agenda be pursued? Of course it cannot be fulfilled without changing public policy and political decision-making. The growing focus on extending deliberative democracy to our existing institutions is welcome. But our approach to governance needs to be broader than this.

There are four, main, overlapping channels of opportunity for developing institutions that can be platforms for everyday democracy, and they need to interact with each other:

O developing public services and local governance as platforms of self-governing communities

O recognising membership and campaigning organisations that can play a clearer role in mobilising political issues and mass participation

O supporting institutions that can be sites of intercultural exchange, dialogue, learning and collaboration

O spreading institutional power more widely and seeking to align power, initiative and responsibility more closely.

But, by definition, these challenges cannot be met through existing structures of government. A distributed vision of democracy and self-governance therefore demands a more wide-ranging approach to its creation. Nonetheless, the major structural opportunity in British government to stimulate more everyday democracy comes from addressing the challenge of localism, and the need to generate a sustainable, legitimate set of local roots for democratic self-governance.[39]

This could be done by:

O creating a local government financial settlement which localises a significant proportion of tax-raising power and matches powers to responsibilities

O embracing a fully fledged vision of neighbourhood governance which delegates management and budgets across key areas

O embedding public deliberation in cycles of institutional development such as trade negotiations, scientific research and innovation programmes, land development and so on

O reshaping public services and careers to make co-production by citizens as important as professional knowledge and performance management currently are

○ initiating co-governance arrangements in local government so that citizen involvement and deliberation is factored into the annual budget-setting processes undertaken by local and neighbourhood government, as in Porto Alegre.[40]

At the same time, we need to explore and promote the democratisation of other sectors and institutions, and to an extent de-monopolise the role of political parties in channelling candidates for democratic representation into institutional life. This might mean:

○ creating rights of initiative and petition which make it possible for a wider range of community and campaigning organisations to develop policy agendas and present them to legislatures and governments in ways that trigger institutional responses; given the power and influence of NGO and campaigning networks in influencing the agenda of governments, their activities should be validated in a way that also demands legitimacy and transparency from them; in other words, these organisations should become partners in governance, and be expected to involve their members in the processes that help to form political and policy agendas

○ promoting models of democratic organisation in the business, public and charity sectors, and supporting them with ownership and governance forms which protect shared ownership and co-governance in law

○ recognising the role of social forums and deliberative networks in global governance domains such as trade and security and seeking new ways to promote deliberation between elite and citizen groupings

○ generating new methods for governments to influence complex systems and learn from decentralised delivery units, and developing new tools with which to engage practitioners and professionals in debating and designing the future.

And in turn these approaches could inform the development of reform options for political institutions which focused on:

O broadening the range of citizen representation in legislative, deliberative and advisory bodies, extending the principle of selection by lot, as Anthony Barnett and Peter Carty proposed for the House of Lords[41]

O seeking to pluralise the composition and culture of political parties so that they draw on wider networks of cooperation and input from social and civic institutions operating in the same communities.

This kind of new institutional capacity, and the ideas needed to nourish and inform them, demand a way of working different from the conventional models of policy analysis and decision-making.

Demos has developed a new way of working in response to these demands. We are still committed to articulating new ideas and using them to start public debate, but our mission can now be summed up as 'building everyday democracy'. We now place as much emphasis on achieving practical influence and learning practical lessons from innovation in every sector, as on working with national government and influencing its policy options.

So, for example, in pursuing a project on the future of Scotland we focused on citizens' engagement with the future, through a town meeting in Nairn. In seeking to understand the new dynamics of scientific and technological innovation and their global impact, we are working with partners from Finland to South Korea, China and India to ground understanding of this new wave in specific cultures and governance approaches.

In looking at new ways to promote independent living for disabled people we are working with Scope, the voluntary organisation, on how to change national policy, local institutions and public culture, simultaneously. In examining the creation of cultural value we are working with the Sage music centre in Gateshead and Tate Modern in London, while in exploring how people participate in local governance structures we are talking to people in the neighbourhoods of South Wales and East Manchester.

Our hope is that this growing body of working knowledge, and the way it is shared among partners and spread across wider networks of learning and exchange, will contribute to the shaping of democratic governance in a new century.

Political leadership and reform is the cornerstone of this process. But its impact will be determined as much by the wider environment on which it tries to act as by the quality of ideas or the integrity of leaders. In the end, we will get the politicians we deserve.

Notes

1   MORI, Social Research Institute, January and April 2005 poll results; available at www.mori.com/election2005/index.shtml (accessed 27 May 2005).

2   J Gray, *Two Faces of Liberalism* (New York: New Press, 2000).

3   See, for example, A Sen, 'East and West: the reach of reason', in *New York Review of Books*, 20 Jul 2000; J Sacks, *The Dignity of Difference: How to avoid the clash of civilisations* (London: Continuum, 2002); A MacIntyre, *After Virtue: A study in moral theory* (London: Duckworth, 1981); D Marquand, *Decline of the Public: The hollowing out of citizenship* (Cambridge: Polity, 2004); J Gray, *After Social Democracy* (London: Demos, 1996); D Goodhart, 'Too Diverse?', *Prospect* 95, Feb 2004; P Singer, *One World, the Ethics of Globalisation* (New Haven, CT: Yale University Press, 2002).

4   See R Williams, 'Formation: who's bringing up our children?', Citizen Organising Foundation lecture, Queen Mary College, University of London; available at www.archbishopofcanterbury.org/sermons_speeches/050411.htm (accessed 27 May 2005); J Sacks, Demos lecture with the Chief Rabbi, 18 May 2005.

5   M Rees, *Our Final Century: Will the human race survive the 21st century?* (London: William Heinemann, 2003); J Jacobs, *Dark Age Ahead* (New York: Random House, 2004); J Diamond, *Collapse: How societies choose to fail or survive* (London: Allen Lane, 2005).

6   For more about this, see: www.mondragon.mcc.es (accessed 27 May 2005).

7   See www.citizensassembly.bc.ca/public (accessed 28 May 2005).

8   S Caulkin on Ricardo Semler, 'Who's in charge here? No one', see: http://observer.guardian.co.uk/business/story/0,6903,944138,00.html (accessed 28 May 2005).

9   See, for example: www.citymayors.com/report/oidp1.html (accessed 28 May 2005).

10 Eurobarometer, Spring 2004; see: http://europa.eu.int/comm/public_opinion/archives/eb/eb61/eb61_en.pdf (accessed 27 May 2005).

11   British Election Study, University of Essex; see: www.essex.ac.uk/bes/ (accessed 27 May 2005).

12   Sociovision; see: www.sociovision.com (accessed 27 May 2005).

13   British Election Survey 2001/02; available at www.essex.ac.uk/bes/index2001.html (accessed 27 May 2005).

14   R Heifetz, quoted in T Bentley and J Wilsdon (eds), *The Adaptive State: Strategies for personalising the public realm* (London: Demos, 2003).

15   G Mulgan, 'Lessons of Power', *Prospect* 110, May 2005.

16   Office of National Statistics, *Time Use Survey* (London: ONS, 2004); of course, this tiny number reflects the fact that many people do not volunteer at all in the traditional sense.

17   For more information see: www.sv.uio.no/mutr/english/scheme.html (accessed 27 May 2005); www.powerinquiry.org/aboutus/links.php (accessed 30 May 2005).

18   Hansard Society Commission on the Communication of Parliamentary Democracy, *Members Only? Parliament in the public eye* (London: Hansard Society, 2005).

19   G Mulgan, T Steinberg and O Salem, *Wide Open: Open source methods and their future potential* (London: Demos, 2005).

20   S Milgram, 'The small world problem', *Psychology Today* 2, nos 60–67 (1967).

21   A Sen, *Development as Freedom* (Oxford: Oxford University Press, 1999).

22   J Fishkin and B Ackerman, *Deliberation Day* (New Haven, CT: Yale University Press, 2004); H Wainwright, *Reclaim the State: Experiments in popular democracy* (London: Verso, 2003).

23   P Ball, *Critical Mass: How one thing leads to another* (London: Heinemann, 2004).

24   S Ringen, *The Family in Question* (London: Demos, 1998).

25   Eurobarometer, Spring 2004.

26   P Bobbitt, *The Shield of Achilles: War, peace and the course of history* (London: Allen Lane, 2002).

27   M Power, *The Risk Management of Everything* (London: Demos, 2004).

28   Bentley and Wilsdon, *Adaptive State*; T Bentley, 'Letting go: complexity, individualism and the left', *Renewal* no 1 (2002).

29   R Cooper, 'Foreign policy, values and globalisation', in T Bentley and D Stedman Jones, *The Moral Universe*, Demos, Collection 16 (London: Demos, 2001).

30   M Hardt and A Negri, *Multitude: War and democracy in the age of empire* (New York: Penguin Press, 2004).

31   Bobbitt, *Shield of Achilles*.

32   C Rosen, J Case and M Staubus, *Equity: Why employee ownership is good for business* (Cambridge, MA: Harvard Business School Press, 2005).

33   M Midgley, *Gaia: The next big idea* (London: Demos, 2001).

34   Ball, *Critical Mass*.

35   R Sampson, quoted in H McCarthy, P Miller and P Skidmore (eds), *Network Logic* (London: Demos, 2004).

36 S Kauffman, *Investigations* (Oxford: Oxford University Press, 2000).

37 J Chapman, *System Failure: Why governments must learn to think differently* (London: Demos, 2002); R Axelrod and D Cohen, *Harnessing Complexity: Organisational implications of a scientific frontier* (London: Basic Books, 2000).

38 S Johnson, *Emergence: The connected lives of ants, brains, cities and software* (New York: Scribner, 2002).

39 One of the best current summaries of how this could happen is G Stoker, *What is Local Government For?* (London: New Local Government Network, 2005).

40 Wainwright, *Reclaim the State*.

41 A Barnett and P Carty, *The Athenian Option: Radical reform for the House of Lords* (London: Demos, 1998).